Sailing

Rita Storey

SEA-TO-SEA
Mankato Collingwood London

This edition first published in 2011 by
Sea-to-Sea Publications
Distributed by Black Rabbit Books
P.O. Box 3263, Mankato, Minnesota 56002

Copyright © Sea-to-Sea Publications 2011

Printed in China, Dongguan

Library of Congress Cataloging-in-Publication Data

Storey, Rita.
  Sailing / Rita Storey.
    p. cm. -- (Know your sport)
  Includes index.
  ISBN 978-1-59771-286-6 (library binding)
  1. Sailing--Juvenile literature. I. Title.
  GV811.13.S76 2011
  797.124--dc22
                              2010003439

9 8 7 6 5 4 3 2

Published by arrangement with the Watts
Publishing Group Ltd, London.

Series editor: Jeremy Smith
Art director: Jonathan Hair
**Series designed and created for
Franklin Watts by Storeybooks.**
Designer: Rita Storey
Editor: Nicola Edwards
Photography: John Cleare, Mountain Camera

Note: At the time of going to press, the statistics in
this book were up to date. However, it is possible
because of the sailors' ongoing participation in the
sport that some of these may now be out of date.

Picture credits
Bigstock pp. 7 and 9; Clive Mason/Getty Images
pp. 17 and 24, Don Emmert/AFP/ Getty Images p.
27; i-stock pp 11, 15, and 26; Shutterstock pp. 6, 8,
and 9. Cover image: i-stock

All photos posed by models. Thanks to Owain
Hughes, Alice Kingsnorth, Robin Kirby, and Claire
Whitehill.

The Publisher would like to thank Tim Cross and the
staff at the Mount Batten Sailing Centre, Plymouth,
UK, for their help. (www.mount-batten-centre.com)

March 2010
RD/6000006414/002

WARNING:
This book is not a substitute
for learning from a skilled
instructor, which is the only safe
way to learn to sail.

Sailing can be dangerous if you
do not take the correct
precautions. If you are spending
time on or near water it is vital
that you know how
to swim.

Contents

What is Sailing?

Sailing can be relaxing and fun or it can be very fast and exciting. Small sailing boats are known as sailboats (or sometimes, dinghies), and sailing in one in a light breeze on a lake can be a relaxing way to spend an afternoon. Racing a customized performance sailboat is a much more exhilarating experience. You have to hang out over the water as you fight to balance the boat and win the race.

All Shapes and Sizes

You can sail single-handedly or with a crew of one or more other people. Sailors take sailboats out on lakes or onto the sea. Sailboats come in a variety of styles and people of all ages, shapes, sizes, and abilities can enjoy sailing them. Some boats are made to suit beginners and families. They are designed more for stability than speed. There are lightweight, faster sailboats for those who enjoy speed and excitement.

If you enjoy fast, exhilarating water sports and do not mind the occasional dip in the water then sailing may be the sport for you.

These young sailors are learning to sail in boats that are very stable and difficult to capsize.

Getting Started

If you'd like to try sailing, the best thing to do is to first contact the American Sailing Association (see page 29 for their web site), who can help you find a sailing club near you. Many clubs offer sessions to people who haven't sailed before to enable them try it out for a few hours to see if they would like to take it further. For those who want to take sailing lessons, there are courses available that are run by qualified instructors. The American Sailing Association (ASA) has schools in 38 states. ASA schools teach sailing to people of all levels of experience, and have a beginner's sailing instructional DVD, called *Sailing Fundamentals*.

City Sailors

Even if you live in a city, there may be opportunities for you to learn how to sail locally. Sailing doesn't need to be an expensive sport to learn.

Races and Regattas

As well as being a relaxing hobby, sailing is an exciting competitive sport. Sailing clubs organize races most weekends throughout the summer and a full day of racing, called a regatta, once a year. Races can be for a class or type of boat or for a mixed group of boats that race against one another using a handicap system (see page 25) to make it fair. Sailing at its highest level is an Olympic and Paralympic sport.

Types of Sailboat

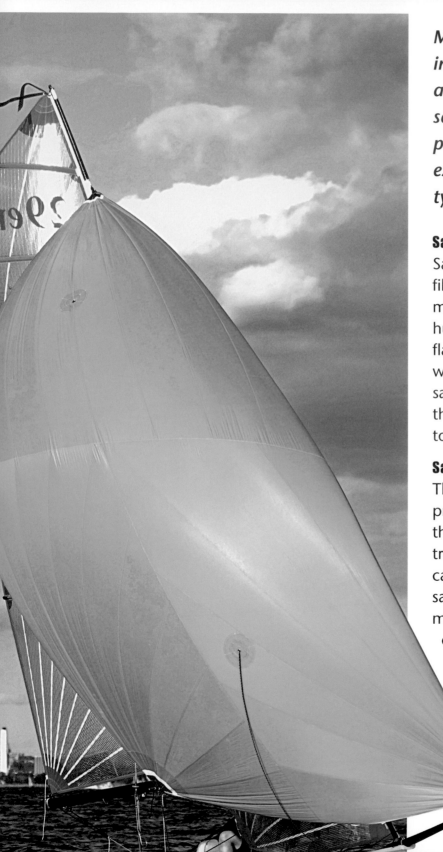

Most young sailors learn to sail in a small sailboat, often called a dinghy. There are cruising sailboats or car top sailboats (see page 9). Once a sailor gains more experience, there are different types of boat for them to sail.

Sailboat Styles

Sailboats can be made of wood, fiberglass, or plastic. The shape of the main body of the boat (called the hull), affects how fast you can sail. A flat, narrow hull will speed across the water but you need to be a competent sailor to keep it upright. A squarer hull that sits lower in the water is less likely to capsize but will not go as fast.

Sails

The larger the size of the sails in proportion to the size of the sailboat, the faster the boat will be able to travel—and the easier it will be to capsize! Some sailboats have only one sail, while others have two sails—a mainsail and a foresail. Sometimes other sails are added for sailing in different conditions. These include spinnakers—the enormous, highly colorful sails that sailors use when their boats have the wind behind them.

◄ Putting up a spinnaker can make a sailboat move a lot faster.

Sailboats for Cruising

Cruising sailboats are designed for leisure sailing. They have smaller sails, which makes them slower and less likely to capsize. Cruisers can still be a lot of fun to sail.

Car Top Sailboats

As their name suggests, car top sailboats can be taken apart and transported on the roof of a car. They are easy to sail and need very little maintenance, and so are used by many sailing schools as a training boat. In the hands of more experienced sailors, they can also be exciting to sail and to race.

Catamarans

Catamarans have two hulls, a high mast, and a large sail. These features mean that they can move very fast on the water.

Performance Sailboats

Performance sailboats, called skiffs, are lightweight and have large sails. The 49er is a two-person skiff that became an Olympic sailing class in 2000 (see page 25). Skiffs are the fastest type of sailboat. They are designed to skim along the surface of the water rather than push through it. To balance these boats, the crew members lean out over the water using a harness attached to the boat by wires. The harness is called a trapeze.

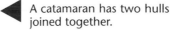
The crew of this 49er skiff balances the power of the wind in the sails by leaning out of the boat on a trapeze.

A catamaran has two hulls joined together.

Clothing and Equipment

When you first begin to sail, you will probably be using a sailing school boat so the only things you need to buy are the right clothes to keep you safe and warm. To start with, you will be able to rent most of what you need from the sailing school.

Warm and Flexible

Sailors who capsize in the winter in ice-cold water are more likely to die of hypothermia than to drown. That makes it vital to have the right type of protective clothing.

Clothing for sailing has been designed to give maximum warmth using light fabrics that are comfortable and easy to move around in.

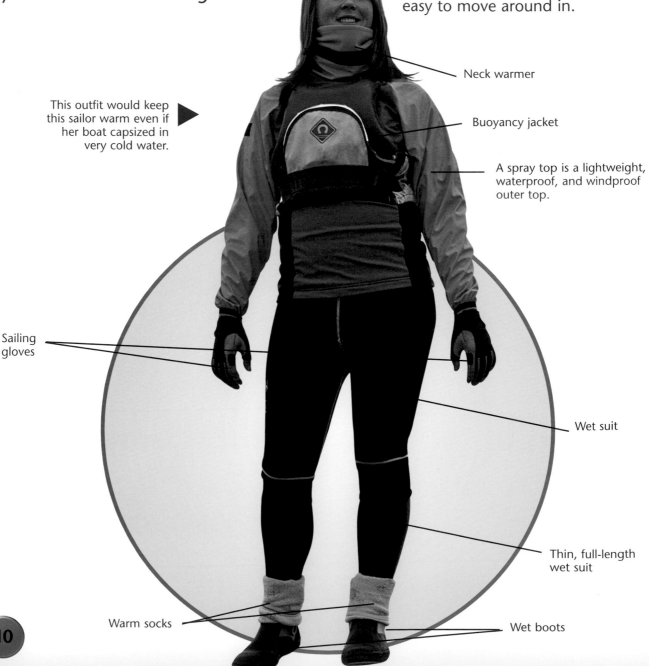

This outfit would keep this sailor warm even if her boat capsized in very cold water.

Neck warmer

Buoyancy jacket

A spray top is a lightweight, waterproof, and windproof outer top.

Sailing gloves

Wet suit

Thin, full-length wet suit

Warm socks

Wet boots

Sailors need to be able to move around the sailboat very quickly. They wear clothes that allow them to do this while keeping them warm.

You will need to wear:

- A waterproof outer layer. This can be a wet suit, a dry suit, or a waterproof top and leggings. Wet suits let in a small amount of water, which warms up next to your body. Dry suits have seals at the neck, wrists, and ankles, which keep all the water out.
- A warm middle layer keeps in your body heat.
- An underlayer. Sailing is an energetic sport and in a hour of moderate exercise, our bodies give off nearly a pint (.5 L) of sweat. Modern materials worn next to your skin draw the sweat away from your skin and stop you from feeling damp and uncomfortable.
- A good pair of sailing gloves keep your hands warm and stop them from getting sore when you pull on the ropes.
- Sailing boots to keep your feet dry. The soles of these boots grip the deck to stop you from slipping.

Safety Equipment

- A buoyancy jacket is a vital piece of safety equipment for anyone who sails, no matter how well they can swim. It must fit properly and not come off if you fall into the water. A buoyancy jacket will not keep you afloat in the same way as a life jacket, but it will help.
- When you are learning to sail, the sailing school will provide a helmet to protect you if you hit your head on the boom (see page 12) as it swings across.

Top Tip

To avoid damaging your wet suit when you are sailing, wear a protective layer over the top. Shorts, a spray suit, or hiking pants will all offer protection.

Rigging a Boat

Before you can sail a boat, it has to be rigged. Rigging means putting together the parts of the boat that have been taken off while it has been in storage.

Before You Start

First of all, you need to make sure that your boat is watertight. All open boats will collect water. Sailboats have holes in the hull to let the water out when you are sailing. The holes are closed with a flap or a plug (called a bung). If these holes are left open, they can let in water. You will need to close the flaps and put in the bungs before you start to rig your boat.

The Boom, Mast, and Sails

A car top boat like the one below ("a Topper") may have its mast and boom taken off so that the boat can be stowed flat on a roof rack. This means you have to put them back on every time you use the boat. Other types of sailboat may be stored with the mast in place.

Some sailboats have only one sail, which is stored rolled around the mast. On other types of boat, the sail is pulled up the mast using a rope called a halyard.

Parts of a Sailboat

Mast The vertical pole to which the mainsail is attached.

Boom The horizontal pole to which the bottom of the mainsail is attached.

Boom vang The connecting piece of rope or wire between the boom and the mast. It stops the boom from rising up.

Bow The front of the boat.

Tiller This moves the rudder to steer the boat.

Cockpit The part of the boat in which the members of the crew sit.

Rudder This goes into the water at the back of the boat and is used to steer the boat.

Launching trailer A frame with wheels and a handle that the boat sits on so that it can be moved around on land.

Stern The back of the boat.

Hull The main body of the boat.

Daggerboard This is a board that is dropped down into a slot in the bottom of the boat when the boat is sailing. It helps to keep the boat upright.

Rigging a Car Top Sailboat

1 Slot the mast into the hole in the hull and lock it in place. Unroll the sail.

2 Clip the boom onto the mast.

3 Attach the sail to the end of the boom.

Boom

Boom vang

Mast

4 Fix the boom vang in place.

5 Attach the rope that controls the mainsail (also known as the mainsheet) to the end of the boom.

6 Slot the rudder and tiller into position. Keep the rudder upright until the boat is in the water.

Launching a Sailboat

Once you've rigged your boat, it's ready to be launched. In a sailing club, you'll probably use a gradual slope built into the water, called a slipway, to launch your boat. The easiest way to get a sailboat into the water is to push it down the slipway on a launching trailer (see page 12).

Launching from a Slipway

1. Push the trailer down the slipway into the water. There needs to be enough water under the boat so it can float. Point the sailboat so the wind is blowing from from bow to stern (this is called "head-to-wind"). Hold onto the sailboat while someone takes the trailer away.

2. Push the daggerboard into the slot in the bottom of the boat. Make sure that the daggerboard is attached to the mast to stop it from falling off if the boat capsizes.

3. Put the rudder down. Move the boat so that the wind is blowing across it. The sail will flap. Climb in. You are now ready to sail away.

Be Prepared

In the summer, when lots of people want to launch their boats, slipways can get very crowded. Before you take your sailboat down the slipway, check that it is properly rigged and ready to sail. Make sure that you have everything you need so that you can launch quickly and smoothly without holding other people up.

You may need someone to help you by:
- Holding the trailer while you float the sailboat off of it.
- Holding the boat while you get into it.
- Putting the trailer back to where it is normally stored to leave the slipway clear for other users.

Be Careful

Never jump into a sailboat when it is still on land. Without the support of the water under it, your weight may make a hole in the bottom of the boat.

There may not always be a handy slipway from which to launch your sailboat. These sailors are carrying their sailboat to launch it from the beach.

Balancing the Boat

To get the best performance out of a sailboat, the helmsman and crew need to work together as a team. They must control the sails, hull, daggerboard, and rudder correctly to keep the boat in balance.

Who Does What?
The helmsman is in charge of the boat. He or she controls the mainsail and the tiller and gives instructions to the crew. The crew sits further forward and controls the daggerboard, the jib (foresail) sheet, and any additional sails that are used.

Balance
A boat that is sailing at a very steep angle will sail more slowly than one sailing at a slight angle. Keeping the boat in balance from side to side can be a difficult job especially in a fast-moving performance sailboat. Both crew members must be constantly aware of where their weight needs to be and change position if necessary. They hook their feet under straps that are fixed to the boat to stop them from falling out as they lean right out over the water.

Boat Trim
The trim is the balance of the boat from front to back. To keep the trim level, the crew members move nearer to the front or back of boat depending on the point of sail (see page 23).

The steep angle of this boat means that the crew will not be able to move at great speed.

16

Sails

It's important to use the right amount of sail for the size of your boat and the conditions in which you are sailing. If you use too much sail in breezy conditions, a sudden gust will tip your boat over. Using too little sail will mean that the boat will not go as fast as it could. On some boats, you can roll the sail around the mast to make it smaller. Other boats have reefing lines attached to the sail. When you pull on these lines it creates a fold in the sail, making it smaller.

Single-handed

If you are sailing single-handedly, you will have to control the balance and trim of the boat and its sails all by yourself.

Pippa Wilson, Sarah Webb, and Sarah Ayton of Great Britain compete on their way to victory in the Yngling class event at the 2008 Olympic Games in Beijing.

▼

Pippa Wilson

Date of birth: February 7, 1986

Nationality: British

Sailing Class: Yngling

2008—Olympic gold medal

2007—ISAF World Championships—gold medal

Sarah Webb

Date of birth: January 13, 1977

Nationality: British

Sailing Class: Yngling

2008—Olympic gold medal

2007—ISAF World Championship—gold medal

2004 Olympic gold medal

Sarah Ayton

Date of birth: April 9,1980

Nationality: British

Class: Yngling

2008—Beijing Olympics—Gold medal

2007—ISAF World Championships—Gold medal

2004—Athens Olympic Games—Gold medal

Sarah Ayton, Sarah Webb, and Pippa Wilson can compete in any weather conditions. They won their gold medals in Beijing in high winds and choppy seas.

Safety

Sailboats are kept upright using the body weight of the crew balanced against the force of the wind in the sails. If your boat isn't balanced, you may capsize. It's vital to know what to do if you capsize and how to get your boat upright again safely.

Righting a Capsized Sailboat

This way of righting a sailboat is called the scoop method. The crew member is scooped up inside the boat as the helmsman pulls it upright. If you are sailing single-handedly, you need to do what the helmsman is doing below.

▼

1 *The helmsman (on the left) knows that the sailboat is going to capsize and is taking action. He is climbing out as the boat tips over.*

Righting a Sailboat

If you capsize, the worst that is likely to happen is that you will get wet. Your buoyancy jacket will help keep you afloat. Sailboats are designed to be righted quickly and easily. Keep calm so that you will be able to think clearly and remember what to do. Practice capsizing and righting your boat when the weather is good. That way you will know what to do and be able to react quickly if you capsize in bad weather or during a race.

2 *The helmsman stands on the daggerboard as close to the hull of the boat as possible and uses his weight to pull the boat upright. The crew member holds onto the inside of the boat.*

Man Overboard Drill

If you sail a two-person sailboat, it is important to practice what to do if one of you falls overboard. Both crew members need to be able to handle the boat so that they can sail back to the person in the water and get him or her back into the boat as quickly as possible.

If you are sailing at a sailing club, there will always be someone on the water in a safety boat to help you if you get into trouble.

Stay Safe

All sailboats are designed with added buoyancy so they should not sink. If you find you can't right your boat, you should stay with it rather than try to swim to the shore. A capsized sailboat is easier to spot than a lone swimmer and you may be farther away from the shore than you think.

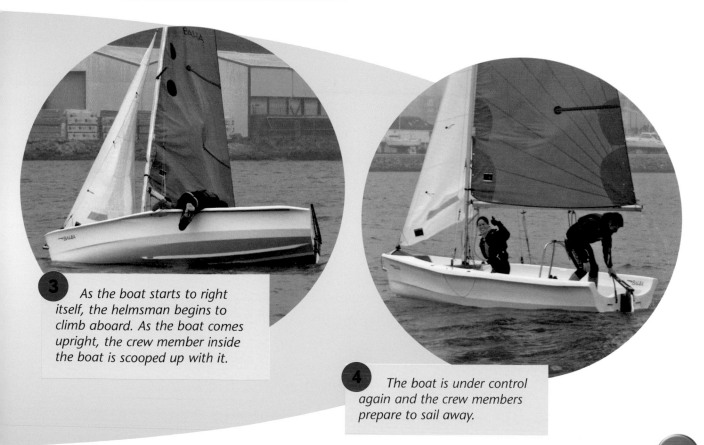

3 As the boat starts to right itself, the helmsman begins to climb aboard. As the boat comes upright, the crew member inside the boat is scooped up with it.

4 The boat is under control again and the crew members prepare to sail away.

Tacking

A sailboat is moved by the wind. As a sailor, you must learn to use the strength and direction of the wind to get the best performance from your boat. If you don't understand what the wind is doing, you may struggle to make any progress or put yourself at risk of capsizing.

Straight Ahead

You cannot sail any boat straight into the wind. If you try to aim your boat toward the wind it will stop and may even start to go backward.

If you want to go straight ahead and the wind is blowing toward you (upwind), you will need to sail a zigzag course. Turning a boat across the wind is called tacking. When you turn the boat, the wind will move the boom from one side of the boat to the other and the mainsail will fill with wind on the other side of the boat. As the boat turns, the crew members have to move across to the other side of the boat to balance it. They also need to adjust the sails on the new course.

Tacking

1 The helmsman decides to tack and shouts "Ready about" as a warning to the crew to prepare to tack.

2 The crew prepares to tack and shouts "Ready." The helmsman pushes the tiller away and the front (bow) of the boat moves across the wind.

The person at the helm who steers the boat is responsible for letting the other crew members know when he or she is about to change to another tack. First, the helmsman will shout "Ready about" as a warning to the crew to prepare to tack. When they are prepared, they will reply "Ready" and the helmsman will push the tiller away from him and shout "Lee-oh" to let the crew know that they are changing direction. They will loosen the ropes attached to the sails to allow the sails to move across to the other side of the boat.

As the boat turns into the wind, all the crew members (including the helmsman) move to the opposite side of the boat to balance it.

Port and Starboard

When you are inside a boat facing the front, the starboard side is on the right and the port side is on the left. When you are tacking, the wind will be blowing over one side of the boat. When it is blowing over the starboard side, you are on a starboard tack and if it is blowing over the port side, you are on a port tack.

Watch Out!

Listen to the instructions from the helmsman. When you change course, the boom will swing across the boat. Be ready to duck if necessary to avoid a bump on the head!

3 *The crew and helmsman move to the other side of the boat. The wind swings the boom to the opposite side of the boat.*

4 *The helmsman pulls in the mainsail as it fills with wind on the opposite tack.*

Jibing

Jibing is the term used for changing course when you have the wind behind you (downwind). It can be a noisy and dangerous maneuver because the boom can swing violently from one side of the boat to the other.

Jibing Safely

If you are sailing with the wind behind you, the boom and the sail will be out over one side of the boat. As you jibe, the stern of the boat will go across the wind and the boom and sails will move across to the other side of the boat. Jibing happens very fast and can make the boat unbalanced even in light winds.

Accidental Jibing

If the helmsman does not steer a steady course when sailing downwind, the boat can jibe accidentally. This can be dangerous because, without any warning, the crew may get hit by the boom as it swings across.

Jibing

1 *The helmsman will shout "Stand by to jibe" to warn the crew of his intention. The crew members reply "Yes" when they are ready.*

2 *The helmsman shouts "Jibe-oh" to let the crew know that the boat is changing course. The boom and sails swing across to the other side of the boat. The helmsman moves to the other side of the boat.*

Direction

When you are sailing, you need to angle the sails in different ways depending on the wind and the direction in which you want to travel.

Close Hauled

The nearest you can get to sailing directly into the wind in a sailing boat is with the boat and sails at an angle of 45° to the wind blowing toward it (upwind).

Beam Reach

On a beam reach, the boat is at right angles to the direction of the wind.

Broad Reach

On a broad reach, the boat is at 45° to the wind with the wind behind it (downwind)

Run

This is when the wind is directly behind the boat (downwind). The sails should be full out.

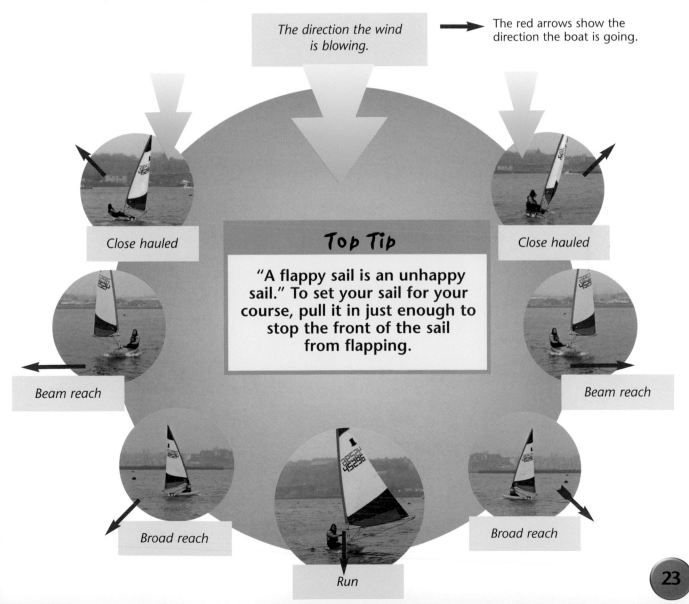

The direction the wind is blowing.

The red arrows show the direction the boat is going.

Close hauled

Close hauled

Beam reach

Beam reach

Broad reach

Broad reach

Run

Top Tip

"A flappy sail is an unhappy sail." To set your sail for your course, pull it in just enough to stop the front of the sail from flapping.

▲ Representing the U.S.A., Anna Tunnicliffe won the gold medal in the Women's Laser Radial sailing class at the 2008 Olympics.

Racing sailboats is a competitive sport at every level, from handicap races at a local sailing club to the top international and Olympic events.

Anna Tunnicliffe

Date of birth: October 17, 1982

Nationality: American

Sailing Class: Single-handed Laser Radial

2008—Olympic gold medal

2009—ISAF Sailing World Cup Series
Sail Melbourne
Rolex Miami

Anna Tunnicliffe was a top sailor throughout high school. She is also a talented athlete. In her final year at school, she won district track championships in the 800 meters and set a new high school record of 2 minutes 17.56 seconds.

One Design

When sailboats that are exactly the same race each other, they are called "one design" classes. The aim of this type of racing is that no boat should have any advantage over another. As a result, the winner should be the crew with the greatest sailing ability rather than the crew with the best boat. People race boats of all types in this way at all levels, nationally and internationally.

Handicap Races

In a handicap event, competitors of different ages and abilities and boats of different classes can compete against one another with an equal chance of winning. A system of time-penalty handicaps adjusts the time each boat takes to finish a course so that the boat that finishes first does not always win the race.

International Sailboat Racing

Sailboat racing worldwide is organized by the International Sailing Federation (ISAF). Sailors compete in national and international races around the world in the run-up to competitions such as the ISAF Sailing World Championships and the Youth World Championships.

Watch Out!

All the sailboats in a race are propelled by the wind. Beware: if another sailboat gets between the wind and your boat, the wind will fill its sails and not yours—and this will slow you right down.

Olympic Competition

Sailing competition at the Olympic Games is organized by classes, or types of boat. In any race, only boats of the same class may compete against one another. The Olympic classes are for single-handed, double-handed, or three-person boats and can be either women's, men's, or open (see below) disciplines.

Open Class

Open classes are for both men and women. In an open class the boats can be modified. There can be differently designed sails and masts. A boat that has been skillfully modified can give its crew the edge over another crew who may have greater sailing ability.

Olympic Dinghy Sailing Events

• 470—Two-Person Dinghy (Men)
• Laser—One-Person Dinghy (Men)
• Star—Keelboat (Men)
• 470—Two-Person Dinghy (Women)
• Laser Radial—One-Person Dinghy (Women)
• Yngling—Keelboat (Women)
• 49er—Skiff (Mixed)
• Finn—Heavyweight Dinghy (Mixed)
• Tornado—Multihull (Mixed)

Racing Rules and Tactics

Once they have some basic experience, most sailors will want to try racing their sailboat against others. Racing adds an element of excitement to sailing. It is a good idea to learn some basic racing rules before you start, to avoid upsetting your competitors.

Racing Rules

A sailing race is sailed around brightly colored marks or buoys that are positioned to make a course. There are 90 different rules that govern racing, but the most important to learn are about who has right of way. Officials at any sailing club that runs races will talk you through what you need to know before you start to race. Knowing the right-of-way rules is particularly important when several boats are going around one of the marks. If you obstruct another boat you may be disqualified. You also need to know the system of sound signals and flags that the race organizers use to communicate with the competitors out on the water.

A Good Start

Your race tactics need to focus on being at the start line in the right place and at the right time. If your boat is miles away from the start line when the race starts, it will make it difficult for you to win the race. Boats that are already sailing at top speed when the start signal goes, will have an advantage over the boats that still have to accelerate up to speed.

However, you need careful timing—if you misjudge it and are over the line at the start signal, you will have to go back and cross the line again. Any boat that does not start correctly is disqualified.

In very light winds, there is a danger of being becalmed away from the start line and unable to move. In these conditions you should stay as close as you can to the start line.

When lots of sailboats are all aiming for the same marks in windy conditions, boats can collide. You need to know what to do to avoid a collision.

Ben Ainslie of Great Britain sails around a mark on his way to winning a gold medal in the Sailing Finn class at the 2008 Olympics.

Trim

To ensure that their sailboat is sailing at its fastest, the crew members need to be in the right place in the boat. Usually it is best to sit well forward when sailing toward the wind and farther back when sailing away from the wind.

Hitting the Mark

Choosing the right course to each racing mark takes practice and experience. To get it right, you have to understand the wind and the changing conditions. Try to see what course other sailors are on so that you can learn from their experience.

Ben Ainslie

Date of birth: February 5, 1977

Nationality: British

Sailing Class: Finn

2008—Olympic gold medal, Single-handed Dinghy (Finn)

2004—Olympic gold medal Single-handed Dinghy (Finn)

2000—Olympic gold medal Single-handed Dinghy (Laser)

1996—Olympic silver medals Single-handed Dinghy (Laser)

Ben Ainslie is an exceptionally talented sailor. He competed in his first Olympics in 1996 when he was 19 years old, taking home the silver medal in the Laser class. He won the world championships in 1998 and 1999 in the same class and then a gold medal in the Sydney Olympics in 2000. He switched to the Finn class in 2002 and won three consecutive world championships. He went on to win an Olympic gold medal in Athens in 2004 (even though a disqualification had left him at the back of the pack and he had to make a remarkable comeback). He won another gold medal in Beijing in 2008.

He was awarded the MBE (Member of the Order of the British Empire) in 2001, the OBE (Officer of the Order of the British Empire) in 2005, and the CBE (Commander of the Order of the British Empire) in 2009.

Record Holders

Event	Gold	Silver	Bronze
Laser class	Paul Goodison Great Britain	Vasilij Zbogar Slovenia	Diego Romero Italy
470 class	Nathan Wilmot Malcolm Page Australia	Nick Rogers Joe Glanfield Great Britain	Nicolas Charbonnier Olivier Bausset France
Star class	Iain Percy Andrew Simpson Great Britain	Robert Scheidt Bruno Prada Brazil	Fredrik Lööf Anders Ekström Sweden

Women's Olympic Champions, 2008 Beijing

Event	Gold	Silver	Bronze
Laser Radial class	Anna Tunnicliffe United States	Gintarò Volungeviciute Lithuania	Xu Lijia China
470 class	Elise Rechichi Tessa Parkinson Australia	Marcelien de Koning Lobke Berkhout Netherlands	Fernanda Oliveira Isabel Swan Brazil
Yngling class	Sarah Ayton Sarah Webb Pippa Wilson Great Britain	Mandy Mulder Annemieke Bes Merel Witteveen Netherlands	Sofia Bekatorou Sofia Papadopoulou Virginia Kravarioti Greece

Open Event Olympic Champions, 2008 Beijing

Event	Gold	Silver	Bronze
Finn class	Ben Ainslie Great Britain	Zach Railey United States	Guillaume Florent France
49er class	Jonas Warrer Martin Kirketerp Denmark	Iker Martínez de Lizarduy Xabier Fernández Spain	Jan-Peter Peckolt Hannes Peckolt Germany
Tornado class	Antón Paz Fernando Echavarri Spain	Darren Bundock Glenn Ashby Australia	Santiago Lange Carlos Espínola Argentina

Glossary

Balance To be equal on both sides.

Becalmed Unable to move the boat because there is no wind.

Boom vang The connecting piece of rope or wire between the boom and the mast. It stops the boom from rising up.

Bow The front of a boat.

Bungs Plugs used to close a hole.

Capsize To turn the boat upside down or on its side.

Crew All the people sailing a boat. Some members of the crew, such as the helmsman, have specific jobs.

Daggerboard A piece of wood, fiberglass, or metal that is dropped down into a slot in the bottom of the boat when the boat is sailing. It helps to keep the boat upright.

Foresail The sail nearest to the front of the boat.

Hypothermia Dangerously low body temperature caused by exposure to cold conditions.

Jib A triangular headsail in front of the mast.

Jibe To change direction by turning the back of the boat through the wind.

Mast The vertical pole to which the mainsail is attached.

Mainsail The sail attached to the boom.

Mainsheet The rope that controls the boom.

Port The left side of a boat, looking forward toward the bow.

Righting Getting a boat upright.

Rudder The vertical metal or wooden plate attached to the stern, the movements of which steer the boat.

Slipway A gradual slope built into the water used to launch a boat.

Starboard The right side of a boat, looking forward toward the bow.

Stern The back of a boat.

Tack To change direction by turning the front of the boat through the wind.

Tiller A piece of wood connected to the rudder. It is used to steer the boat.

Trim The balance of a boat from front to back.

Web Sites

www.asa.com
American Sailing Association is the leading authority on sailing instruction and sailing schools in the U.S.A. You can learn to sail through the network of ASA certified sailing schools with certified sailing instructors. ASA Certified Students can go from basic sailing lessons to advanced sailing courses, enjoying sailing experiences in the United States and around the world.

www.kidscamps.com/
Click on "sailing" to search for a summer camp where you can learn to sail in the U.S.A, Canada, or worldwide.

www.sailing.org/isafsailing worldcup
The official web site of the International Sailing Federation has up-to-date information about all the ISF events. Click on the "Connect to sailing" button to find details of how to get started in sailing.

www.sailcraft.com
Sailcraft helps sailors of all levels explore exquisite locations along the West Coast of Canada. They introduce people who have never been on a boat before to sailing but also challenge advanced sailors with programs including ocean racing.

Note to parents and teachers: every effort has been made by the Publishers to ensure that these web sites are suitable for children, that they are of the highest educational value, and that they contain no inappropriate or offensive material. However, because of the nature of the Internet, it is impossible to guarantee that the contents of these sites will not be altered. We strongly advise that Internet access is supervised by a responsible adult.

Index